Naval Heritage in the W

G000021803

by Andy Endacott

PART II

MAGNIFY-CIENT WORK IS BEING DONE BY **OUR NAVY**.

Cover picture

A 'Kent' class cruiser built by Vickers of Barrow in 1928, of 10,000 ton displacement. She was at the final stages of the Battle of the River Plate in December 1939, replacing *HMS Exeter*, which had been badly damaged, but in fact never needed to use her guns. When used as a film star years later in the film version of the Battle, she had no guns to fire, because in 1949 she had become the Royal Navy's first trials cruiser for guns, missiles and Denny-Brown fin stabilisers, and was therefore continually altering her equipment. Incidentally, she was the first ship I worked on in 1954 as a shipwright liner. My job was to sketch and order new cable deck bonnets on two main decks. This cruiser was finally scrapped at Newport in November, 1959.

THEY ALL LOVE JACK

JACK COMES HOME.

The ships of old England they travel afar
All manned by the best of good sailors they are.
Each happy as a lark, and gallant and brave,
With heart warm as sunshine yet strong as the wave.

ISBN *0.9511527.1.8*
First published: *June, 1987*
Text © D L ENDACOTT 1987

Published by D L ENDACOTT, 58 GLENHOLT ROAD, PLYMOUTH, and printed by Penwell Ltd., Parkwood, Callington, Cornwall.

INTRODUCTION

Welcome back for the second phase of the pictorial coverage of the Naval Heritage of the West. It has been a difficult but very enjoyable task to collate the wealth of photographs and information so generously given to enable me to continue the story, and I hope that my enthusiasm in bringing together some of the important events, both Service and civilian, between 1900 and 1950, has rekindled many happy memories. I have attempted to update and enlarge on the areas covered in Book 1, with some valuable help from Official sources and private collections.

Amateur photography during the period was generally limited to the Box Brownie camera, and official photos were normally "Classified", especially during the War Years. It has been absorbing—and amazing—to find so much valuable information carefully preserved in both official and private collections, especially when the modern attitude is so often "It's old and useless—throw it away".

We live on an island, surrounded by seas which protect us, allow our Naval protectors to move with ease, the Merchant Navy to bring in our supplies and our Fishing Fleets to catch our food, so we are rightly proud of our Maritime heritage.

In this volume I have included the Approaches to the River Tamar, and additional branches of the Service, i.e. Royal Marines, WRNS, Fleet Air Arm and Shore Training Schools. There are glimpses of VIPs and various activities associated with the Dockyard and the Navy. I have indulged myself by introducing some comic cards and advertisements of the period. How sad that this style of advertising has long since disappeared.

The years between 1900 and 1950 saw the change from Wooden Wallers to Dreadnoughts and Battleships used in both World Wars. The mighty force of the Big Guns was introduced and with these we controlled our seas. The Navy still required improvements and, after many frustrating trials, developed the Flat Tops, to take aircraft out to sea for reconnaisance and bombing runs. Throughout this time the Dockyards were also building ships and Devonport produced many famous names and various types from submarine to aircraft carrier. Naturally, officers and men had to be retrained to man the greatly-improved Navy, and many "stone-warships" were built as Training Schools. The West Country continued to play an important role in the development of the Navy, and has done so to the present time.

Since this period the big ships and guns have been phased out and replaced by smaller and faster vessels with missiles. Electronic technology, jet aircraft and helicopters and nuclear submarines have become the Navy's right arm and were all put to the test in the Falklands Campaign. These modern items will be covered in the final edition of the Naval Heritage, period 1950 to 1986.

My grateful thanks to Admiralty House, Mount Wise, Mrs Williams, Syd Goodman, Jim Broad and AVA Torpoint, for the material and information they provided, and to all those who so willingly aided this project.

© D L ENDACOTT
58, Glenholt Road,
Plymouth PL6 7JD   June '87

Note   Apologies are offered for the photographic error on Page 12 of Book 1. The ship was *HMS Duke* and not *HMS Queen* as stated.

HMS Rodney, on display at Navy Week in 1936, alongside the main Devonport Dockyard berths, with her guns elevating towards Torpoint. Her wartime service included involvement in the 'Sink the Bismark' action. Built by Cammell Laird in 1922-27 she and *Nelson* were to have been to a design tonnage of 48,000 but because of Naval Treaties were reduced to 33,900 tons.   *S. Goodman Collection.*

CARE AND ATTENTION

The Naval Hospital is sited in Stonehouse and was opened in 1762. Between 1800 and 1814 over 48,500 seamen and marines were received and a great proportion returned to service. Here we see a group of Nursing Sisters (circa 1898) who gave so much care and attention to the wounded and sick from the ships of war. *Courtesy of Naval Hospital Archives.*

This group of veterans of many campaigns is posed around the Sundial at the Royal Naval Hospital. The design of the wheelchairs indicates that these men were from the Wooden Wallers' era, (circa 1898.) *Courtesy of Naval Hospital Archives.*

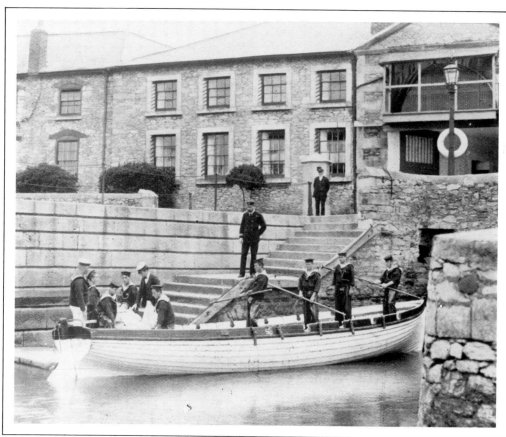

At the rear of the Hospital was a creek, where the patient had to be brought by boat from his ship in the *Sound* or the *Hamoaze*, having been lowered over the side in a canvas cot (circa 1898). Just after the first World War, patients were brought to the Hospital by modern motor transport, thus dispensing with the sometimes very rough sea journeys.

Central Photos.

Another method of moving the patient was in this two-wheeled cradle hauled by Naval Hospital attendants.

Devonport, Royal Sailors' Rest

Xmas Cheer

CAUSE AND EFFECT

The Royal Sailors' Rest, erected by Miss Agnes Weston and her friend Sophia Wintz, at a cost of £80,000, on the site of six public houses. The original building was opened in 1876 and by 1889 had mushroomed to provide 800 cabins. After her death in 1918, admirers added a further block as a memorial, giving the building its complete grandeur as shown. Unfortunately it was destroyed during the Second World War in 1941.

Families and Associations at home still remembered the sailors on the high seas, and dispatched food parcels, which were gratefully received.

DECORATIVE FITTINGS

This Royal figurehead is from a 101-gun vessel and has been named *Royal Adelaide* in this 1960 photo. It has since been revealed that it really came from *HMS Cambridge*, 1858, and was originally called *Windsor Castle*. Both these vessels had spent many years moored in the Hamoaze. Now—to complicate records even further—the figurehead is situated outside the Wardroom at Manadon College and called *HMS Victoria* (120 guns, the last three-decker). She really has had an interesting career!

This beautiful lady, baring her upper body to the wind, was from the *Aurora*, 1861, a 50-gun frigate. These figureheads were usually part of an all-over scheme of decoration from the bow to the greatly carved sterns.

Even on the early iron ships such as this—*HMS Victoria,* 1887, of 10,470 tons and carrying 2 x 16.5'' breech load, 1 10-inch and 12 6-inch BL guns—there was still a requirement for a decorative wood carving on the bow. *Syd Goodman Collection*

The crew polishing the guns (16''). The decorative brass plates blanking the barrels are called 'Tampions' and protect the rifling against the weather. The tampion bears the ship's crest, and similar plaques are displayed on the bridge and mounted on boards for display and souvenirs.

THE SOUND YOU CAN SEE

O the fair town of Plymouth is by the seaside
The Sound is so blue and so still and so wide,
Encircled with hills and with forests so green,
Like a crown of fresh leaves on the head of a queen
O dear Plymouth town and O blue Plymouth Sound!
O where is your equal on earth to be found?

Plymouth Sound was no safe harbour when gales blew from the South. So John Rennie, a great engineer, was consulted, which resulted in the commencement in 1812 of the building of the breakwater, which was completed in 1840. J. Whidbey supervised the building and resided in this house called "Bovisand House" in the valley under Madame Hill.

C. Gill Collection.

The breakwater is 1700 yards long, with the ends drawn back slightly. It cost a million and a half pounds, and used 3 million tons of granite and 4 million tons of limestone. Special railway lines and wharves were made to help in this enormous project.

This defence against the sea had turned the Sound into a safe harbour. Other defences against enemies were constructed either side of the entrance to the Sound, which included the large fortress shown here, standing 100 yds behind the breakwater. It was 144ft long, 114ft wide and designed to have fourteen 12.5 inch guns and four 10 inch guns. It soon became obsolete, and was mainly used as a Naval Signal Station.

Ships leaving the Dockyard and passing across the Sound soon drew admiring crowds. Here we see *HMS Rodney*, 1936, passing the Banjo Pier on the Hoe foreshore, and another Class of Battleship coming out of the narrows. *Syd Goodman Collection.*

HMS Illustrious, with paying off pennant, about to enter the narrows past Devil's point, on a traditional rainy West Country day. Whatever the weather, these occasions still brought relatives and friends to the Rusty Anchor vantage point to watch the ships.
Syd Goodman Collection.

VICTUALLING THE FLEET

From Devonport Column.

PLYMOUTH SOUND.

This grand view was made possible in 1824, when Plymouth Dock was renamed Devonport. A Doric Column 124ft high was built as a lasting memorial and access to the top was made. In the middle of the view is the Naval Signal Station at Mount Wise (Book 1, page 42 refers). To the left of the view can be seen the Royal William Victualling Yard, consisting of ''a massive block of buildings, built of granite and containing Stores of vegetables, lime juice, clothes, bedding for the supplying of Her Majesty's ships''. In the Cooperage, tanks and barrels were made by the hundreds, and the steam-driven machinery in the Bakehouse could grind 1,000 bushels of corn on the Millstones within 10 hours. There was also a brewhouse and a butchery.

Serving out a day's fresh meat ration on *HMS Talbot*. This ship was at Devonport, and one pound of fresh meat was issued to each man per day (circa 1896). At sea, meat rations were—every other day one pound of salt pork, on one alternate day one pound of salt beef and on the other day ¾ pound of preserved meat. *Courtesy of Royal William Yard.*

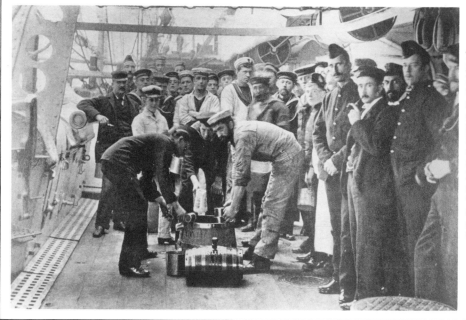

Testing the grog on board *HMS Sovereign*, (circa 1886). The sailors' rum was drawn from the spirit store in presence of an officer at seven bells (11.30am), put into a breaker and taken on deck, where it remained under a sentry until, at half past twelve, it was mixed in a ''grog tub'' with 2 or 3 parts of water and then served out. Half a gill of rum was allowed to each man. *Courtesy of Royal William Yard.*

Aboard *HMS Renown* in 1906, an orderly queue of messmen line up for their allowances of grog for their respective messes, and here have been requested to pose for the photographer.

Teetotallers were allowed some compensation, the money value of the rum, or its equivalent in cocoa and sugar.

SHIPBUILDING AT DEVONPORT

The launching of the battlecruiser *HMS Lion* in South Yard, 1910. With a complement of 1,000 officers and men, she later fought at the Battle of Jutland and became the Flagship of the battle cruiser Squadron at that action.

On 23 September, 1942, Lady Forbes performed the ceremony of launching *HM Submarine P326* (afterwards called *Tudor*) at South Yard, Devonport. With a complement of 68, she operated in the Far East during the War and was finally broken up in Scotland 1963. *Crown Copyright Reserved.*

HMS Terrible was the only Aircraft Carrier to have been built and completed in a Naval Dockyard. She was launched by Mrs Duncan Sandys on 30 September, 1944, on No. 3 Slipway, South Yard, and was of displacement 14,000 tons and 695ft long and 80ft beam. Handed over to the Royal Australian Navy in 1948 and renamed *HMAS Sydney*. Broken up in South Korea 1975. The fixed tower cranes were fitted in 1938, and replaced the 'prop and job hoists' as shown on page 16.

Crown Copyright Reserved.

This is an example of the style of graphics produced in 1924 in a souvenir programme, giving infinitely detailed flamboyance to the work. Possibly the work of a draughtsman with additional artistic talents.

The *Athel Duchess*, a 13,000 ton Norwegian owned tanker, was damaged by a mine and broke in two but the stern section was saved. The Admiralty were anxious to get 'repayment work' in order to use the Dockyard resources to the full and maintain full employment. This fore end was built and then launched by Mrs Hvistendahl, wife of the owner, on 9th December, 1947, on No. 3 Slip, South Yard. The stern had been towed down from South Wales and was married up at Devonport. The two white arrowheads are the locating points for the join-up.

Naval Base—Photo Section.

Will it be the last? Launch of *HMS Exeter* by Lady Madden at Devonport Dockyard. In view of the great naval reductions, it may be years before a similar scene is witnessed at Devonport. *Quote: Doidges Annual 1930.*

"WE'RE THUMBS UP IN THE NAVY"

The ships of Old England, of metal or wood,
Of steam or of sail, they are equally good.
Old England's strong walls they ever abide
Our safety as ever—as ever our pride.

A Floating Dock is a floating watertight structure serving the same purpose as a dry dock, and it is capable of being submerged sufficiently to receive a floating ship by admitting water into the "pontoon tanks" which form the bottom of the dock. Here we see *HMS Resolution* in dock.

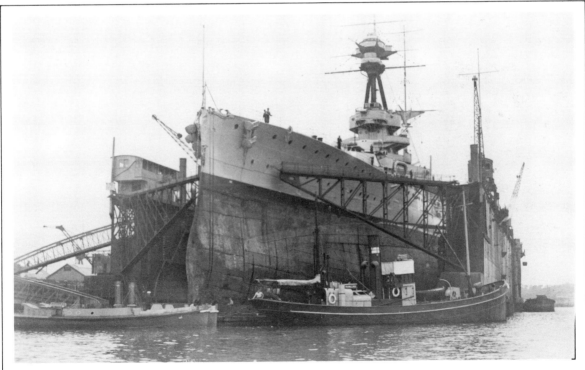

Another 'R' Class battleship, *HMS Ramilles*, in the Floating Dock at Devonport. Both these vessels were 624ft long and 88ft 6 inches wide and of 28,000 ton displacement. Note also the anti-torpedo bulge which was introduced and increased the beam to 101ft.

TORPOINT CROSSWAYS

Torpoint Ferry foreshore (circa 1900) with the training ships *Implacable* and *Lion* moored off Thankes, Torpoint. The craft in front of *Lion* were ''Temperly transporters'' used in coaling ship. The *Lion* was a 2nd rate 80 gun launched at Pembroke 1847, and converted to screw with 400 HP engine in 1849, and sold in 1905.

Torpoint Ferry pontoon with steamer *Lady Beatrice* alongside. The steamer operated between Torpoint, North Corner and Rattery Quay, in conjunction with the floating bridge. The cruisers in mid-river are of the *Arrogant* class, one of these being the Devonport built *Arrogant* herself, laying in reserve (circa 1905). Finally broken up in 1923.   *AVA Torpoint.*

Eve of demolition of more buildings on the Devonport foreshore approach to the Torpoint Ferry in 1931. One can see the neatly packed hard core being laid and a sheeted-down Steam Roller that is being used. An interesting advert can be seen on one of the Ballast Boxes. *AVA Torpoint.*

More slipway work being progressed for the Torpoint Ferry, alongside the Boat House used by naval officers for their sailing dinghies and yachts. *AVA Torpoint.*

DOCKYARD ENTRANCES AND APPROACHES

St Levan's Gate entrance to the Northern end of the Dockyard, originally built in 1896 and resited in this position in 1900. The high mast structure contained the 'start-and-stop-work' bell under a cover. Around 1950 a fire broke out in the North Yard Boat House at 5.00am. The Plymouth Fire Brigade raced to help and arrived at the gate to find it shut. The Duty policeman quoted the Admiralty Memo, which stated that the doors were only to be opened between 6.00am and 11.00pm. The fire engine eventually had to drive away, enter the Dockyard through the Albert Gate entrance and pass the inside of St Levan's Gate on the way to the fire.

This scene, outside St Levan's Gate in the early 1920's, has not really changed very much, except that the electric tramcar with its lines and overhead wires has disappeared.

KEYHAM GATE DEVONPORT

This impressive arched entrance was the main approach to the Keyham section of the Dockyard. To the left, near the trees, is the end of Sparrow Park (see page 36, Book 1). Immediately inside were 3 dry docks, clocking stations and cycle racks. The tram double rails and points in the road were a menace to cyclists, as the cycle wheels could drop into the tracks if they were not watching carefully.

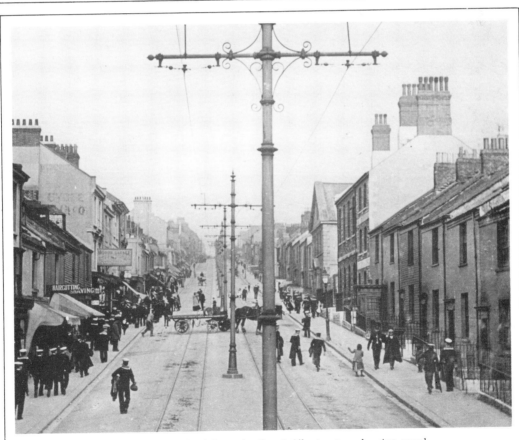

View up 'Navy Row' from the Royal Albert gates, showing naval personnel making their way home or on leave. The central pylons supported the electrical overhead wires for the electric trams. Some of the shops on the left still exist, but the right lower half of the road was bombed during the war and the site has since been absorbed into the Dockyard. *Central Photos.*

RIVER MOVEMENTS

The Torpoint floating bridge, passing under the stern of a second rater 74-gun ship of the line. The ferry was built in 1834 at Hockings Yard, Stonehouse, to the design of James Meadows Rendel of Okehampton.

Central Photos.

See opposite below.

The Nelson-period ship *Implacable* being floated out of No. 4 Dock in 1936 after a lengthy refit. She is attended by tugs *Aetna*, *Atlas* and *Retort*. A North Corner waterman hovers nearby, on the lookout for useful bits of timber. *Implacable* was used at Devonport, Falmouth and, finally, Portsmouth as a training ship before being scuttled at sea with full naval honours in 1949. *AVA Torpoint.*

HMS *Defiance* being towed to the ship breakers in June, 1931, by the dockyard tugs *Rover* (ahead) and *Pert* (alongside). She had been launched at Pembroke Dock in 1861 and had been completed as a 91-gun screw ship of the line. In 1884, at Devonport, she was fitted out as a torpedo school and was moored off Wearde Quay, Saltash, in 1886. She is shown passing *HMS Argus*, which was laid down at Beardmore's on the Clyde, as the Italian liner *Conte Rosso* in 1914. Requisitioned by the Admiralty, she was completed as an aircraft carrier, and survived until 1946.
AVA Torpoint.

NAVY WEEK

"THAT'S THE CAPTAIN'S LOUD-SPEAKER FOR GIVING HIS ORDERS."

A naval 2-badge Able Seaman giving the vulnerable Joe Public and family some awe-inspiring nonsense information to take home.

The *Rodney's* main wood-covered deck being invaded by civilians, during the period of Navy Week, August 1st—August 8th, 1936. Above the gun, a breeches buoy is being used to demonstrate the method of transferring people at sea.

Royal Marine band playing to the public during an open day. Note the wooden deck planking, and breakwater plating acting as a barrier from the Band. The gooseneck crane and cabin can be seen in front of the coal heap and coaling gantry. (See Book 1, pages 26/27 refer). *G. Brooks Collection.*

Miss "Future" with gas mask, the centre of attraction during Navy Week at Devonport. *Quote: Doidges Annual 1930.*

SALTASH PASSAGE

The Royal Albert Bridge Inn at Saltash Passage was originally called the Dock Inn, but the name was changed when the bridge was built. This annual wagonette outing in 1908 drew in friends from the Wheatsheaf at Saltash and many serving naval ratings and Royal Marines.

M. Ware

Looking from Saltash across to the Brunel Railway Bridge, with a steam-hauled passenger train arriving. At the far river-bank is a pair of houses, one of which was called 'Ferndale' at Riverside, St Budeaux.

This family group of Longs, Hills and Enda-cotts was taken in the doorway of 'Ferndale' in 1933. The small boy (centre) is the author, with grandparents and other relatives. The occasion was the funeral of my grandfather, who was ex Yeoman of Signals and driller in the Dockyard. My father and uncles at that time were serving Royal Marines and Naval personnel. My own son is now working in the Naval Dockyard, Devonport.

A NAVAL DISASTER

"Torpedoed him in his Engine-room—did yer?

Well if I git hold o' yer—Ye'll need a new Propeller!"

Ship's crew leading the Breakwater crew in 12-oar cutter race. Note the Q ships and destroyer, laid up after the 1914-18 War, up-river past the Saltash Railway Bridge. *M.Ware.*

NAVAL COLLEGES *'Stone Warships'*

ROYAL NAVAL ENGINEERING COLLEGE, KEYHAM, DEVONPORT.

The College at Keyham has trained junior engineer officers since it was opened in 1880. Because of the ever-increasing numbers of officers to be trained, an additional site was obtained at Manadon, north of Plymouth, in 1935. Hutted accommodation, hangars and workshops were built there. In 1946 both Keyham and Manadon were given the name *HMS Thunderer*.

" The Luck of the Navy."

Members of the Photographic Club of the Royal Naval Engineering College, Keyham, in 1891, with their wooden tripods and bulky plate cameras, holding still for a long-aperture exposure. Little did they realise that in 90 years time photography would achieve such high speeds, using minute cameras—and in colour. How could they even imagine photographic competitions set on such subjects as 'through the lens of a submarine periscope', when they had never even seen a submarine! *Central Photos.*

HMS Britannia was one of the eight King Edward VII class battleships of 15,630 tons displacement, length 453ft and beam 78ft. They were the first to be fitted with balanced rudders (see page 22, Book 1). *Britannia* was sunk by a U-boat in 1918.

H.M.S.BRITANNIA

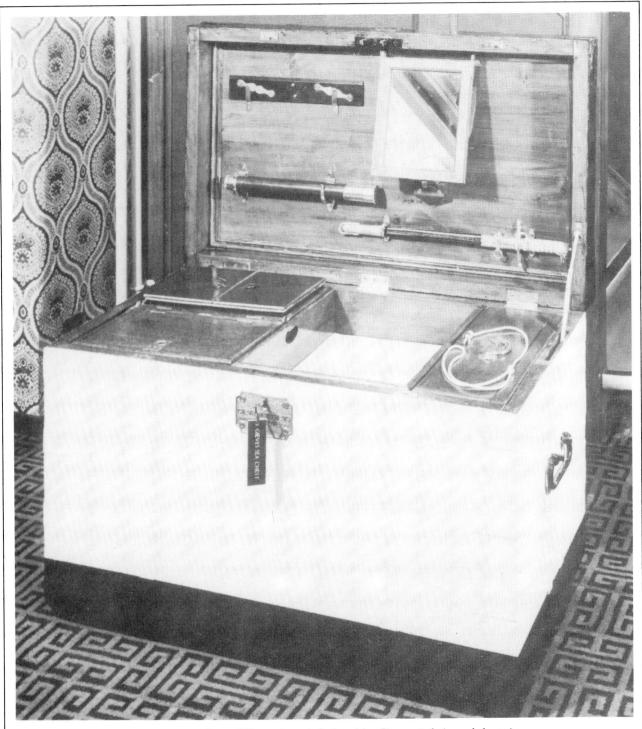

The cadet sea-chest, 1903, made and designed by Gieves at their workshops in Portsmouth. It held the midshipman's dirk, watch-keeping telescope and parallel rule, and there were trays for toilet fittings and clothing. The chest acted as a complete wardrobe and safe and bore the owner's name on an engraved brass plate.

Courtesy of Gieves & Hawkes.

H.M.S. "Britannia," for 36 years the Training Ship for Britain's Naval Cadets. Now being dismantled to make Munitions of War, Gift Souvenirs, and Memorials.

"Britannia" Souvenirs

"CAPSTAN" DOUBLE INKSTAND.
11 in. long × 8 in. wide × 4 in. high
Polished dull Antique Finish . . . **21/-**

DITTY BOX, 12 in. long, 7½ in. deep,
9 in. wide. Polished dull Antique Finish **55/-**

"CAPSTAN"
SINGLE INKSTAND
4½ in. × 5½ in. base **12/6**

BLOTTERS
to match, 5 in. by
3 in. high. Complete **10/6**

*HANDY TROUGH
FOR BOOKS.*
In Polished Teakwood, 13½ in. long,
5⅝ in. high, 7½ in. wide . . **10/6**

When the War is won and over, when the Fleet has done its work, Souvenirs of the old "Britannia" will have even greater sentiment and interest than now.

Jellicoe, Beatty, Sturdee and all but the very youngest Naval Officers of to-day learned the rudiments of their glorious calling on the "Britannia."

To a Naval Friend you could send no Gift more acceptable than a reminder of his happy training days. Amongst the range of "Britannia" pieces you will find something suitable for *every* Gift occasion.

Each article possesses Novelty and Utility. And even the least costly Gift embodies the quiet dignity of Hughes, Bolckow Craftsmanship.

Four typical examples are illustrated here. Other "Britannia" Souvenirs consist of Candlesticks, Chairs, Stools, WAR SHRINES, GARDEN SEATS and Tables, Blotters, Photo Frames, Walking Sticks, Smokers' Ash Bowls, Caskets, Jacobean Stools, etc., in Oak, Mahogany, Teakwood, etc.; also a few Cigarette and Cigar Boxes, Fern Pots, Barrel Jugs, Coal Scoops, Candlesticks, etc., in Copper; Hearth Stands, Door Porters, Door-knockers, etc., in Gunmetal; and old-world Garden Figures in Lead.

(National Requirements will prevent the repetition of the Copper, Gunmetal and Lead Souvenirs when the present stock is disposed of).

"BRITANNIA" SOUVENIR BOOK FREE ON REQUEST
illustrating almost 100 pieces. If unable to call at our West-End Showrooms, please send a post-card for it.

WEST-END SHOWROOMS
At 10, Dover Street, you are invited to make leisurely inspection of "Britannia" Souvenirs, and Indoor and Outdoor Furniture made from the Timbers of this and other Famous Ships.

HUGHES·BOLCKOW & CO·LTD
10 DOVER STREET **W**
Battleship Breakers   Blyth . . . .
Northumberland   **1**

Dover Street 'Phone :   " Regent 2297."   [L.H.]

See opposite page.
This unique publication, issued by Gieve, Mathews and Seagrove, Ltd. (circa 1910), was the mail order catalogue to the serving naval officer. It contained illustrations of available stock, prices and sizes of uniforms, leisure wear, sports equipment, etc. Gieves kept details of measurements of accounts customers, so that when orders were transmitted ahead, the required garments could be made to await the arrival of the officer concerned. *Kind permission of Gieves & Hawkes.*

See opposite page.
The Royal Naval College at Dartmouth was built between 1900-1905. (Before this time officers trained aboard the wooden-walled *Britannia* and *Hindostan*, moored on the River Dart). It suffered bomb damage in 1942 and closed down for normal training use until 1946, but was used by other service groups temporarily during that period. This fine College has produced first-class officers for many countries' navies as well as our own.

TRAINING SCHOOLS

Boys from the training ship *Impregnable* in cutters, laying off the *Impregnable* Steps. They are tossing oars in salute, possibly to a visiting Captain, as his gig is in the foreground. The steps were built to provide access to the playing field which was adjacent to the Cremyll Obelisk. (circa 1904). *AVA Torpoint.*

HMS Defiance, torpedo school, moored off Wearde Quay, Saltash. The ship in left foreground is *Inconstant*, which joined *Defiance* as an accommodation ship in 1920. To the right is the *Defiance* of 1861. A parade ground and boat sheds were built ashore, and the GWR built a small station, Defiance Halt, for the convenience of personnel living ashore. The establishment at Wearde Quay was disbanded in 1930, and re-established with other vessels off Wilcove in the same year. *M. Ware.*

HMS Defiance, electrical and torpedo school, moored off Wilcove, where the establishment was sited from 1930 to 1955. This photograph shows, left to right, HMS Andromeda, launched in 1902 as a first class protected cruiser of 11,000 tons. Ahead of her is the Vulcan, of 6,620 tons, built in 1889 as a carrier for small torpedo boats. On the right, outside the Vulcan is Inconstant, built as a screw frigate in 1862. Reputed to be the fastest vessel under sail in the Navy of her time. These ships remained off Wilcove until disposed of in 1955.

P. Rouse
Collection.

ROYAL MARINES

DURNFORD STREET AND R. M. BARRACKS, STONEHOUSE.

Stonehouse consisted mainly of Government Institutions and offices, all on a very large scale. Such a place was the oblong Square of the RM Barracks, built in 1782, containing apartments for the ranks at the front and the officers at the sides, accommodating approximately 750 men. The Marine band performed daily on the parade ground, much to the enjoyment of the residents in the neighbourhood. The building stands proudly still today, but the numbers using it have been greatly reduced.

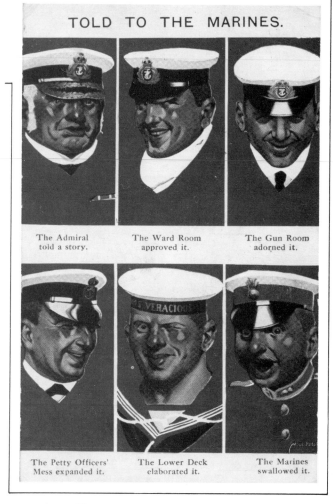

TOLD TO THE MARINES.

The Admiral told a story.

The Ward Room approved it.

The Gun Room adorned it.

The Petty Officers' Mess expanded it.

The Lower Deck elaborated it.

The Marines swallowed it.

Our Dreadnoughts.
THE JOLLY.

ERNEST IBBETSON

G   R

All Dashing High-spirited
YOUNG HEROES
Who wish to obtain GLORY in the SERVICE
have now the finest Opportunity,
of their Country, that enterprizing respectable Corps
by entering that enterprizing respectable Corps

THE ROYAL
MARINES.

Every one must be well aware, that this Honorable Corps, possesses Ad-
vantages superior to any other under, the Crown. Good Quarters whilst on
Shore; on Board, plenty of Beef, Pudding, and Wine after Dinner. Even these
Advantages are trifling when compared to the inestimable one

PRIZE MONEY.

Remember the Gallooms; when the Private Marine made sufficient Prize Money to render him-
self and Family comfortable for Life.
Remember these Times; may returning to the head Quarters of the BRIGHT, or to Sergeant
Lieuse no Time! therefore, in Marines, commanded by LIEUT. Gen. BRIGHT, or to Sergeant
of the Plymouth Division of Royal Marines, BRNIOL, where every attention will be paid to them.
GRIBBLE, at the BLUE BOWL, Division of Royal Marines, BRNIOL, where every attention will be paid to them.

Eleven Guineas Bounty
SEVEN YEARS SERVICE,

Sixteen Guineas
UNLIMITED SERVICE.

Boys 5 Feet, Eight Guineas, limited Service,   Twelve Pounds, unlimited
NOW OR NEVER,   ENGLAND FOREVER
The Bringer of a Recruit will be handsomely rewarded.

GOD SAVE the KING:

The King's Squad of Royal Marines, marching in the V.E. Victory parade, 1945, in front of the City Museum. The buildings shown here have now been replaced by the Polytechnic College, Sherwell. *Mrs Williams, ex WRNS.*

The Royal Marine Cadets on their first public march, during the Plymouth Victory Parade, 1945, passing proudly down beside the ruins of St Andrew's Church.   *Mrs Williams, ex WRNS.*

King George VI with Queen Elizabeth visited Plymouth and Stonehouse after the bombing in March, 1941. Here His Majesty is inspecting the Royal Marines, assembled on the parade ground at the R. M. Barracks, Stonehouse.

Mrs Williams, ex WRNS.

Inspection of the Plymouth Royal Marine Police detachment by Admiral Sir Robert L. Burnett, KCB, KBE, DSC, LID (C in C Plymouth) and Commander Clayton, Commandant of the Royal Marine Police, outside Admiralty House, South Yard—May 1948. Do any of you Dockyard or Navy people still remember the fearsome presence of 1128! *Crown Copyright Reserved.*

THE WRENS

A "Flock of Wrens" gathered at Flagstaff Steps to receive a briefing from a senior Naval Officer. In the background are some Flower Class corvettes, in particular K79 Petunia, April 1954.
Crown Copyright Reserved.

Their Majesties arrived at Admiralty House, escorted by police car and WRNS outriders. The Queen accompanied by Lady Forbes, inspected the WRNS boat crews at Flagstaff Steps, and finally boarded the boat, which was flying her own Royal Standard. She travelled up-river to be disembarked at the RN Barracks Pier, where she proceeded to the Barracks to inspect 2000 WRNS on parade. May 1942.
Crown Copyright Reserved.

The Special Drill Squad of Royal Marine WRNS, marching past the saluting platform alongside the damaged shell of St Andrew's Church, Plymouth, during the 1945 Victory Parade. They were the winning Squad at *HMS Drake*, 1942-43, competing against all in the South West Command.

Mrs Williams, ex WRNS.

SUNLIGHT SOAP

IN HOME WATERS.

WORDS could not express more perfectly all that is told in this picture. Neither can words fully convey the nation's gratitude to our gallant navy. Therefore, we leave our illustration to express all we would say of Jack, of his good wife, bonny son and happy home. Likewise we think that the Quality and Efficiency of SUNLIGHT SOAP with the satisfaction and leisure they bring are also best expressed in this illustration of

SUNLIGHT IN HOME WATERS.

£1,000 GUARANTEE OF PURITY ON EVERY BAR.

The name Lever on Soap is a Guarantee of Purity and Excellence.

LEVER BROTHERS LIMITED, PORT SUNLIGHT.

S 306—84a

Here we see examples of usage of Naval personnel in advertising for household products. There was a far greater awareness of the Navy and its potential as an advertising medium to the families at home just after the First World War. *Punch Magazine 1917.*

H.M.S. "Indomitable" thriving on

Bird's Custard

"It is a way they have in the Navy"
to enjoy the best of everything

and there is no more popular dish than BIRD'S Custard with the Handy Man. His healthy appetite delights in the great nutriment, the rich creaminess, and clean fresh flavor of this delicious Custard.

As only the best is good enough for the British Navy, only the best — and that is BIRD'S should be selected for family use.

Extract of a letter from a Gunner with the Fleet: – "We only realise it's Sunday because we always have Custard for dinner."

BIRD'S Custard is sold in Pkts., Boxes and large Tins.

SAILORS DON'T CARE!

AND NEITHER WOULD YOU

IF YOU HAD BEEN REARED ON

FARLEY'S RUSKS

BABY NEEDS THEM NOW

Sold in Sealed Cartons of Eleven Rusks for Tenpence by all good Bakers, Chemists and Grocers. Free Samples from the Model Factory in Plymouth.

Local Advert, 1936.

TRANSPORT

A horse, ranking in the Navy as an AB, whose name was Bob and was carried on the books of the Royal Naval Barracks. The driver, an AB, was a stableman, groundsman and gardener. *AVA Torpoint.*

Fred Cole with prize-winning horse "Sam". Mr Ware had the tenancy of the St Budeaux Station Yard. Shell cases were made in the Midlands factories, delivered to the Yard, and transported to the Bull Point Armament Office during the First World War. In 1915 1,309 tons were moved, and 4,052 tons in 1916, and as the Yard got busier in 1917, William Cleaves, a carrier from Camel's Head, was called in to help. *M. Ware.*

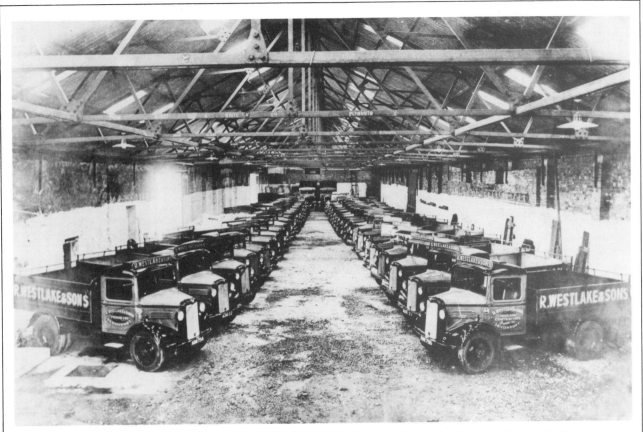

R. Westlake, Haulage Contractors, had a large number of working horses, many on hire to the Dockyard. The firm eventually changed to motor transport and this new fleet of Bedford lorries was delivered to Tamar Wharf in the early 1930's. Some of these Bedfords were very soon undertaking contract work in the Dockyard. In the back of the building can be seen two Dennis iron-wheeled vehicles. *Courtesy of Mrs W.S. Paddon.*

The Dockyard's own passenger service, (circa 1910), which ran at half-hourly intervals the full length of the Yard. The carriages were constructed in the Dockyard, and consisted of an open truck for tool boxes and five box-cars. The first three cars were converted to carry workmen, the fourth was sub-divided into two for Chargemen and Recorders and Petty Officers and Chief Petty Officers, and the fifth was divided into three compartments for Subordinate Officers, Commissioned Officers and—the most sacrosanct of all—Principal Dockyard Officers. *Central Photos.*

ROYAL REVIEW—TORBAY 1910

The Royal Yacht *Victoria and Albert,* with the Royal Family aboard, moving through the lines of ships. The Review had originally been programmed to take place at Mount's Bay, Penzance, a few days earlier, but an approaching storm forced the armada of ships to move to the sheltered area of Torbay.

A total of 230 ships, including 37 battleships, lined up for review. It was estimated to be £100 million-worth of ships, crewed by over 50,000 officers and men. An uninvited participant at the Review was a sole aviator in his bi-plane, who circled over the fleet—much to the concern of the sea-captains who lay powerless below. Since this time the fleet has taken advantage of the Torbay anchorage and held reviews in 1922 and 1969.

Also on review was a selection of 'B' and 'C' Class submarines, who were to prove many years later a bigger menace to the Fleet than any aircraft. The 'B' Class were the first to be fitted with fore hydroplanes and were 143ft long, with a crew of 13. The 'C' Class were then fitted with two periscopes and had a crew of 16.

During 1908 the 'D' Class submarine was introduced, which was 165ft in length with a crew of 27. They were the first British submarines to be fitted with wireless, and some were even fitted with a 2-pounder gun.

V.I.P. VISITS

Prime Minister—Right Hon. Winston S. Churchill—visited Plymouth in May 1941 and inspected the damage caused by enemy bombing in the Dockyard, R. N. Barracks and the City. Shown walking aboard *HMS Trinidad*, which had been built and launched at Devonport in 1939, and was being fitted out. Unfortunately the ship, which was armed with 12 6-inch and 8 4-inch guns, 3 aircraft and 1 catapult, was sunk within one year of entry into service. *Crown Copyright Reserved.*

Here Dockyard 'maties' express their pride that the Prime Minster has visited them at South Yard during his long West Country morale-boosting tour.

Crown Copyright Reserved.

The visit of Her Royal Highness the Duchess of Kent in May 1940 to officially open the new YWCA building at Mount Wise. Accompanying Her Highness is Lord Astor and the C in C, Admiral Sir Martin Dunbar-Nasmith, VC, KCB, passing through the section of WRNS personnel.

Crown Copyright Reserved.

The Queen preparing to board the official launch manned by WRNS, watched by a crowd of Dockyard employees and friends. Already aboard were Lady Spencer, Lady Forbes, Superintendent Welby, WRNS, and Captain Gandell, RN. This was part of the VIP tour of the Plymouth and District area made by their Majesties in May 1942.

Crown Copyright Reserved.

His Majesty the King arrived at Millbay Docks in the Royal train from London at 10.30am on 2 August, 1945. The Commander-in-Chief went out with him in the Royal Barge to *HMS Renown*. Later the Commander-in-Chief met the President of the United States at Queen Anne's Battery and took him in his barge to *USS Augusta*. His Majesty the King entertained the President—Mr Harry S. Truman—to luncheon in *HMS Renown*, bade him farewell as he sailed in the *USS Augusta* for the United States, and subsequently left Millbay in the Royal train at 5.30pm. *Crown Copyright Reserved.*

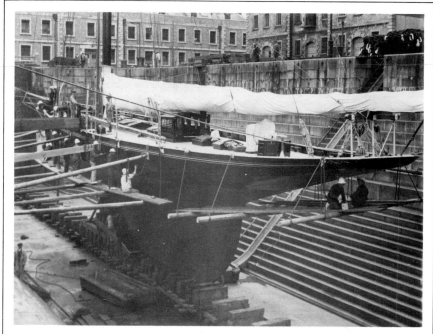

The Royal Yacht *Britannia* receiving hull maintenance in a dry dock, South Yard, 1924. She was the most noteworthy racing yacht of her time, with a gross tonnage of 221, length o.a. 122.5ft and beam 23.5ft. King Edward VII bought and sold her many times, and in her earlier years she won 147 prizes in 219 races. In 1930, with the King on board, she recorded her 200th victory in racing. The rig was altered many times and finished up with a Bermudian style.

NAVAL HUMOUR

BIG GUNS

Now from the tower bridge we can see the area covered by these three triple-barrelled gun turrets. *Rodney* and *Nelson* were the only British battleships to be fitted with 16-inch guns.
G. Brooks Collection.

Looking back aft at the two forward turrets of *HMS Rodney* in an almost maximum elevation position for these huge 16-inch calibre barrels, with the tower bridge in the background.

Here we can clearly appreciate the size of these open Barbette guns of 13.5-inch calibre, on an ''Admiral Class'' such as the *Anson*, (circa 1889). These are breech loaded guns and weigh 67 tons each.

Here we can easily compare the size of the Big Guns—4 at 15-inch—on *HMS Queen Elizabeth* with this view of officers and crew assembled over the main weather deck areas and guns.

A full broadside from a capital ship, where 15-inch shells are projected over 35,000 yards across the horizon at the enemy. The smoke was usually preceded by a flash of light, which during night engagements would locate the enemy's position.

THE FLEET AIR ARM

A flight deck packed full of Fairey Seals on board *HMS Glorious* during her Mediterranean Cruise 1933-34. Note the standby vessel astern, ready to rescue ditched aircraft.

H.M.S. EAGLE WITH AIRCRAFT UP

HMS Eagle, at 22,600 tons, was the largest aircraft carrier in the Royal Navy. She was originally being built as a battleship for the Chilean Navy, but when the 1914 War commenced she was bought from the Chileans and converted to a carrier. The Fairey Flycatcher is last away and later will have the nerve-racking problem of landing again.

To assist this Fairey Flycatcher, of 29ft span and 23ft length, the naval landing staff grabbed hold of the wings to bring her eventually to a halt. The *Courageous* and *Glorious* were sister ships and not in those days fitted with arrester wires.

Here on board *HMS Furious* in 1935 we see a Hawker Nimrod about to land (above), with its hook hanging down ready to engage one of the wires stretched across the deck. (Below). The wire is beginning to take the load, reducing the plane's movement forward.

The return to the mother Carrier is sometimes fraught with problems. Here a Blackburn Ripon standard carrier-borne torpedo bomber had a fire emergency as she landed back on *HMS Glorious*, 1933, during the Mediterranean Cruise.

BRITAIN'S NEW FLOATING AERODROME.

HMS Courageous, 1928, which had been converted into an aircraft carrier at a cost of over £2 million. This view was taken as she left Devonport for her steaming trials.

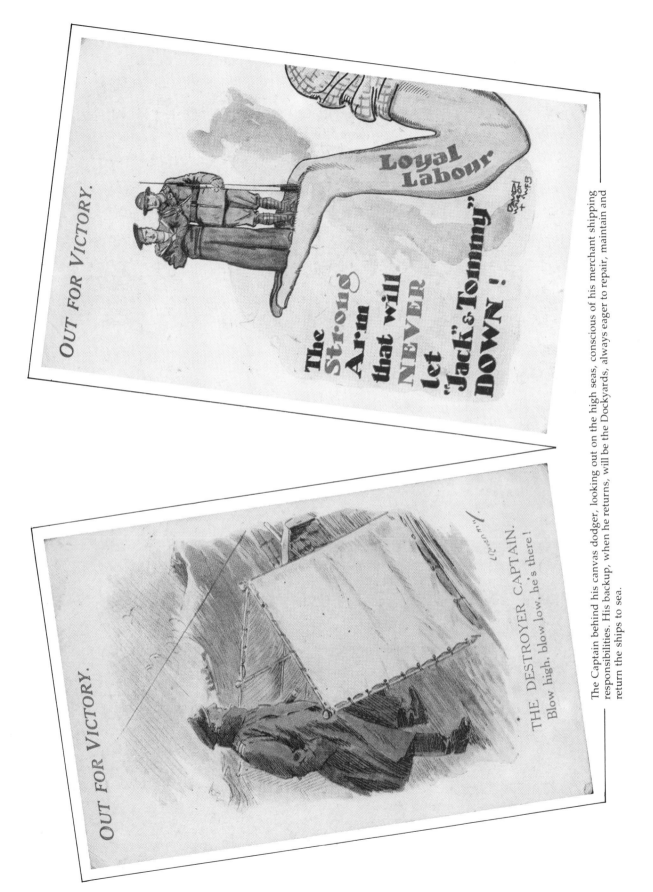

OUT FOR VICTORY.

The Strong Arm that will NEVER let "Jack & Tommy" DOWN!

Loyal Labour

OUT FOR VICTORY.

THE DESTROYER CAPTAIN.
Blow high, blow low, he's there!

The Captain behind his canvas dodger, looking out on the high seas, conscious of his merchant shipping responsibilities. His backup, when he returns, will be the Dockyards, always eager to repair, maintain and return the ships to sea.

FAMOUS SHIPS

The *Amethyst* arriving back at Devonport on November 1st, 1949, after her "River Yangtse Incident". Officers and crew were welcomed by the Board of Admiralty and given a civic welcome and luncheon by the City of Plymouth. The ship eventually returned to active service in the Korean war, 1951, and was finally taken by the shipbreakers, Messrs Demellweek and Redding of Sutton Harbour, in 1957.

C. Gill Collection

HMS Exeter arriving in Plymouth Sound, thence on to her home port of Devonport, where she was built in 1929, having fought against the pocket battleship *Graf Spee* in the River Plate. They were welcomed back by Sir Winston Churchill, the First Lord of the Admiralty, who joined the ship in the Hamoaze before she docked on 15th February, 1940. After a lengthy refit following extensive damage she left Devonport to join the Home Fleet and head for the Middle East. Alas, in March 1942 she was scuttled by her crew after a valiant action against the Japanese in the Dutch East Indies. Also anchored alongside Drake's Island is the destroyer *Vindictive*.

Crown Copyright Reserved.

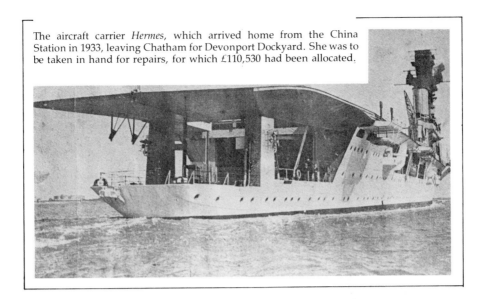

The aircraft carrier *Hermes*, which arrived home from the China Station in 1933, leaving Chatham for Devonport Dockyard. She was to be taken in hand for repairs, for which £110,530 had been allocated.

HMS Vanguard arriving in No. 10 Dock at Devonport, to prepare for her Tilt Test, July 1946. She had just completed sea trials, which would explain her much damaged hull paint-work.   *Syd Goodman Collection.*

Even the famous eventually arrived "up the Trot" to await disposal. Here we see *Renown, Unicorn, Valiant* and *Resolution* in 1946, alongside some torpedo boats   *P. Rouse Collection.*

The first sailor to be demobilised at Devonport on 18th June, 1945, receiving official thanks for a job well done.   *Crown Copyright Reserved.*

Back Cover Picture
An updating of 'the boyhood of Raleigh'. The old sea-dog relating some of his voyages on the high seas, and engagements with the enemy.